I Am Affirmations

The Power of Words

Peter Mulraney

ISBN: 978-0-6488119-5-4

Introduction

I am affirmations are statements of belief. We use them all the time, often unthinkingly, to reinforce our beliefs about who we are.

Spend some time listening to the I am statements you make. Write them down so you can see them. If you're like most people, you'll be shocked by the number of negative I am statements you make about yourself and repeat to yourself every day.

This is a book of positive I am affirmations you can use to remind yourself who you are and what you're really like.

Don't just read each affirmation. Say each affirmation out loud and repeat it to yourself frequently as you go about your day.

When you first start working with affirmations you will meet some resistance. We all do, thanks to our social conditioning which teaches us to think about ourselves in less than supportive ways. Fortunately, you can change the way you think about yourself.

As you work with these affirmations, you'll hear the voice of your inner critic. Saying positive affirmations your subconscious doesn't agree with will flush out your hidden beliefs about who you are and what you're like as a person.

Don't try to suppress that voice. Acknowledge it and let your hidden beliefs become visible so you can release them, stop saying them, and overwrite them with new positive I am affirmations.

IAM a miracle

I AM amazing

IAM
assertive

IAM attentive

IAM attractive

IAM authentic

IAM beautiful

IAM blessed

I AM caring

I AM compassionate

IAM complete

IAM confident

I AM
courageous

IAM creative

IAM
curious

IAM decisive

IAM energetic

IAM enthusiastic

I AM eternal

IAM exciting

I AM free

IAM friendly

I AM funny

I AM generous

I AM gracious

I AM grateful

IAM happy

IAM helpful

I AM here

I AM holy

IAM
imaginative

IAM
incredible

IAM innovative

IAM
inspirational

IAM intelligent

IAM intuitive

IAM
inventive

IAM jovial

I AM joyful

I AM kind

I AM lovable

IAM mindful

IAM motivated

IAM
nurturing

IAM

one with source

I AM

open

I AM optimistic

IAM
peaceful

I AM playful

IAM poised

IAM positive

IAM powerful

IAM productive

IAM
prosperous

IAM

refreshing

I AM relaxed

IAM sacred

IAM safe

I AM spirit

splendid

I AM

IAM
spontaneous

IAM
successful

IAM
supportive

IAM thankful

IAM
the light

IAM thriving

IAM trusting

IAM valuable

I AM valued

I AM vibrant

IAM welcoming

I AM well

I AM willing

Some parting thoughts

When I started working with I am affirmations, I wrote them out using a paint brush and acrylic ink in an artist sketch book, and flipped through the pages every night.

If you enjoyed working with the I am affirmations in this book, consider writing your own book of I am affirmations. The format doesn't have to be elaborate. It's the words that count.

If you're interested in reading the thoughts of a modern-day mystic, visit my blog www.petermulraney.com where you can subscribe to my monthly newsletter 'Insights from a crime writing mystic' and download a free copy of **A Question of Perspective**.

Thank you for buying the book.

Peter Mulraney

Other Titles by Peter Mulraney

Writings of the Mystic
Sharing the Journey: Reflections of a Reluctant Mystic.
A Question of Perspective
My Life is My Responsibility: Insights for Conscious Living
Beyond the Words: Reflections on I Am Affirmations
Mystical Journey: A Handbook for Modern Mystics
Inspector West series
After
The Holiday
Holy Death
Whistleblower
Twisted Justice
The East Park Syndicate
Stella Bruno Investigates series
The Identity Thief Collection
The Fallout Collection
Novella
The New Girlfriend

Living Alone
After She's Gone
Cooking 4 One
Sanity Savers
Living Alone (Collection)
Everyday Business Skills
Everyday Project Management
Everyday Productivity
Everyday Money Management
Sharing the Journey Coloring Books
Mandalas
Mandalas by 3
Sharing the Journey Coloring Journals
Sharing the Journey Coloring Journal
Sharing the Journey Coloring Journal ~ Discovery
Sharing the Journey Coloring Journal ~ Reflection